A MANGIA
(LET'S EAT)

A SOUTHERN ITALIAN COOKBOOK
Family Secrets and Timesaving Tips

Compiled and Edited by
Marilena Amoni and Don Ryan

Amoni

*Buon'Apetito!
Marilena*

WESTCOM PRESS

New York   Los Angeles   Washington DC

Westcom Press
2101 N Street, NW
Suite T-1
Washington, DC 20037

westcomassociates@mac.com

18 17 16 15 14 13 12 11 1 2 3 4 5

ISBN: 978-0-9835003-6-0

Library of Congress Number: 2011943781

Dedication

This book is dedicated to Marco Amoni as a small token for the many life lessons he shared with family and friends during his life. "Pop" was a self-made man and a loving husband, father, grandfather, uncle, and friend. With his wife and business partner, Antonetta Amoni, he lived life with gusto, happiness, and success at every level.

Most of the recipes in this cookbook are for traditional dishes from Sant' Arsenio, the little village in a fertile valley in southern Italy called Vallo di Diano where Marco and Antonetta were born. After moving to the U.S. in 1951, Grandma and Pop owned two restaurants on Long Island (*Italian Gardens* and *Roman Gardens*) before entering the catering business, where they served tens of thousands of guests at *Gigi's*, a famous catering establishment in Westbury, NY.

What makes this book special are the secrets it shares for making traditional Italian dishes faster and easier based on the collected wisdom of Grandma and Pop, other family members and close friends, all fabulous cooks who also came to the U.S. from Sant' Arsenio. With a keen eye for observing the world, based on 40 years in the restaurant and catering business, Pop loved to say, "There's a better way – find it." This book does just that.

In loving memory of Marco Amoni, a great cook
himself, who loved family, friends, good food, and
fine red wine for under $5.00 a bottle or box.

Acknowledgements
Recipe, What Recipe? I'm Italian!

This book began with the modest aim of capturing Grandma and Pop's favorite recipes and cooking tips for their grandchildren, Elizabeth, Emily, Daniel, and Michael. Many of these recipes were handed down by mothers and grandmothers to daughters over generations in southern Italy. As word of the book spread, several of Grandma's family and friends who also came from Sant' Arsenio volunteered their favorite recipes as well as their own tips to simplify and streamline cooking. This book therefore offers the collected wisdom of many exceptional cooks, both in documenting previously unwritten recipes for traditional dishes from the Italian countryside and sharing "tricks of the trade" to simplify their preparation.

We thank the following gifted cooks for sharing their recipes, secrets, and tips:

- Antonetta Amoni (Grandma)
- Mary Episcopo
- Anthony Coiro
- Louis Coiro
- Flora Fasciani
- Carmelina Costa
- Franca Sacco
- Marilena Amoni
- Ginger Amoni

And we thank our friend Michael Vezo for inspiring us to make this a real cookbook and for his assistance with publishing.

Some of this book's dishes credit by name the person who contributed the recipe. Other recipes pay tribute to family members and friends or are named after places of significance to Grandma and Pop.

A Word about Ingredients and Proportions

Experienced cooks from Sant' Arsenio do not use written recipes for most dishes. Moreover, when asked to explain how to prepare a dish, they typically use vague terms and instructions such as, "Cover the bottom of the pan with oil," "Throw in a handful of flour," and "Add whatever spice you like." We have pressed the cooks for details, and have done our best to estimate proportions for ingredients and spell out instructions step by step. Nevertheless, it's possible that our proportions may be slightly off. Use your best judgment and common sense, and feel free make adjustments as you see fit.

In a few cases, our recipes call for ingredients by brand name. This does not constitute an endorsement of the brand, but rather our experience with simplifying the recipe and its preparation. Feel free to make substitutions as you see fit.

Table of Contents

Grandma's Secret Cooking System

Everyone agrees that Grandma is an exceptional cook. Her Italian dishes are simply delicious. But what makes Grandma a truly remarkable cook is how amazingly fast she can create a multi-course meal. The magic to her cooking system is actually quite simple:

- 3 Core Ingredients You Must Prepare in Advance

- 20 Things You Must Keep on Hand

    - Checklist #1 – 10 Items for your Pantry

    - Checklist #2 – 5 Items for your Refrigerator

    - Checklist #3 – 5 Items for your Freezer

- 10 Tips that Take the Mystery out of Italian Cooking

If you follow Grandma's simple system and the recipes in this book, you too can make healthy and delicious Italian dishes with amazing speed and ease.

Three Core Ingredients You Must Prepare in Advance

Before you rush ahead to try any recipe, you must first make and keep on hand three core ingredients to speed the preparation of many dishes:

1. **Minced Garlic in Olive Oil** (see step-by-step instructions on page 5) – If you begin any recipe by peeling and mincing a clove of garlic, you are wasting valuable time. Mincing garlic is a messy, unpleasant job that needs to be done in bulk once or twice a year. With fresh minced garlic in your fridge – and a backup supply in your freezer – you are ready to roll with any dish.

2. **Tomato Sauce** (see recipe on page 17) – In addition to topping off a bowl of spaghetti, tomato sauce is a core ingredient in many other recipes. You should *always* have tomato sauce on hand. Follow the recipe to make a big batch and then save in both the refrigerator and freezer in serving-size plastic containers with screw tops with the contents labeled. Whenever you run out of tomato sauce, make another batch. (Don't even think about buying tomato sauce at the store, because Grandma's recipe is so much better!)

3. **Marinara Sauce** (see recipe on page 16) – The other core ingredient in many meat dishes is marinara sauce, which tenderizes chicken, pork, round steak, stew meat, and other cuts. Once again, follow the recipe to make a big batch and save in both your refrigerator and freezer in serving-size plastic containers with screw tops. Make things easy for yourself by labeling the content of these containers.

Things You Must Keep in Your Pantry, Refrigerator, and Freezer

In addition to the three core ingredients that you make in advance, use the following checklists to ensure your pantry, refrigerator, and freezer are well stocked. If you follow these simple checklists below, you will be able to make 90% of these recipes without a special trip to the store.

Checklist #1

10 Things You Should Always Have in Your Pantry

1. Boxes of pasta of various sizes and shapes – Keep an eye out for a sale and stock up. (See tip #7 on page 6 for specific suggestions.)

2. Extra virgin olive oil – Keep a big jug in your pantry and a smaller bottle with a pour top within easy reach of your cooktop.

3. Canned crushed tomatoes for making tomato sauce – Look for the 102-ounce can (or an equivalent number of smaller cans) so you can make a big batch to save in the fridge and freezer.

4. Canned diced tomatoes for making marinara sauce – Once again, shop for the big cans and make a big batch to save in the fridge and freezer.

5. Crushed red pepper – Buy a large container with a sprinkle top and keep it handy.

6. Canned tuna – Buy the less expensive dark tuna, which has more taste.

7. Canned beans (kidney or cannellini) and either canned or frozen green peas

8. One bag of dry lentils

9. One bag of onions

10. Italian breadcrumbs

Checklist #2
5 Things You Should Always Keep
in Your Refrigerator

1. Minced garlic in olive oil – Make this in bulk once or twice a year so that it's ready to begin every dish that calls for garlic. (See tip #1 on page 5.)

2. Tomato sauce already prepared – When you run out of tomato sauce, it's time to make another batch to speed the preparation of scores of recipes. (See recipe on page 17.)

3. Marinara sauce already prepared – This serves as a tenderizer for many meat dishes. (See recipe on page 16.)

4. Basil and parsley in olive oil – Make this in bulk once or twice a year with fresh basil and parsley, once again to give you a running start on many recipes (see page 5 for instructions.) (See tip #2 on page 5.)

5. Grated cheese – Romano cheese, which is made from sheep's milk is more flavorful than parmesan cheese, which is made from cow's milk. Grandma recommends a blend of parmesan and romano.

Checklist #3

5 Things You Should Always Keep in Your Freezer

1. Extra sealed jars of minced garlic (see page 5)

2. Extra sealed jars of tomato sauce (see page 17)

3. Extra sealed jars of marinara sauce (see page 16)

4. Frozen chicken scallipini filets (see page 46)

5. Frozen meatballs (see page 52)

You may have noticed some repetition in the lists above. Please let that serve as a reminder of the importance to keep on hand an ample supply of the three core ingredients: minced garlic, tomato sauce, and marinara sauce. Each of these is critical to Grandma's cooking system.

10 Tips that Take the Mystery out of Italian Cooking

1. **How to prepare and store minced garlic** – Buy a large jar (e.g., one quart) of fresh, peeled garlic cloves. Mince all the cloves in a small food processor to a very fine, almost pasty consistency. Fill small plastic freezer jars with screw tops with the garlic and fill with olive oil. Wait a few minutes for the olive oil to settle and add more to cover the garlic paste. Keep one in your refrigerator and freeze the rest. Make minced garlic in bulk once or twice a year.

2. **How to prepare and store basil and parsley** – Buy several large bunches of fresh parsley and an equal amount of fresh basil. Wash, clean, and throw away the stems. Cut very finely with a knife on a chopping board and mix together in a small plastic freezer jar with screw cap. Cover with olive oil, let settle, and add more oil to cover the leaves. This basil/parsley mix is a fast and effective way to spice up many dishes.

3. **How to sauté garlic step by step** – A majority of both meat and vegetable dishes begin with "Sauté garlic in olive oil," so you need to have this down pat. The trick is not to burn the garlic – and the secret to that is having the next ingredient ready to add to the pan as soon as the garlic is done. Begin with a generous amount of olive oil in the bottom of a heavy pan. If the recipe doesn't specify the amount, a good rule is one tablespoon per person. Put the flame/heat on *low*, add the minced garlic, and stir almost constantly as soon as the garlic begins to sizzle. When the garlic changes color from white to yellow – it only takes about one minute – it's done and time to immediately add the next ingredient so that the garlic doesn't burn.

4. **How to sauté onions step by step** – The process for sautéing onions is similar to garlic, but it takes longer and requires higher heat. Once again, have the next ingredient ready before you begin. Pour olive oil into the pan, turn the heat on *medium* and add the sliced/chopped onion. Stir periodically so that it doesn't stick. The color change of the onion is the clue to when it's done, changing from white to translucent and then to golden. When the onion turns a golden color (in about 5-6 minutes), it's done and time to add the next ingredient.

5. **Don't be afraid of garlic and red pepper** – Garlic and red pepper add spice and zest to almost all southern Italian vegetable and meat dishes, so make these two of your best friends. Once garlic is sautéed it loses its strong odor and adds rich flavor, so feel free to use a heaping portion when the recipe calls for garlic. Similarly, don't be shy when the recipes calls to "Add red pepper to taste." Buy a large container of crushed red pepper that has a flip-top and large holes in the top allowing you to shake the pepper flakes into the pan – and keep this at the front of your spice shelf. Many dishes improve with 3-4 good shakes of crushed red pepper. If you put too much, your guests will let you know. Note that "pepperincino" is red pepper that's been ground into a powder; it's generally used as a garnish at the table, such as for sprinkling on pizza or pasta, but usually not for cooking.

6. **Keep your olive oil handy** – If you enjoy cooking Italian dishes, buy extra virgin olive oil in a large jug to have a good supply on hand. Keep a large glass container of olive oil with a pour top by your cooktop so that you can quickly add this frequent ingredient. Olive oil is used for almost all dishes, except for frying, which calls for vegetable or canola oil.

7. **Select the right pasta for your dish** – Note that our recipes that call for pasta often suggest a specific size or shape of pasta to complement the rest of the dish. So be bold at the grocery story – especially when pasta is on sale – and buy a variety of shapes: pastina and tortellini (for soup); ditalini (with beans and peas); rotini with tuna sauce; spaghetti or linguini (with shrimp); etc. As a general rule, figure 80 grams of pasta per serving, except 100 grams when you are having spaghetti (because everyone always seems to eat more spaghetti for some inexplicable reason). Two favorite brands of pasta are Barilla and Rigatoni. Many types of pastas are also available in whole wheat, which is a healthier than plain pasta but takes slightly longer to cook.

8. **Don't overcook the pasta!** Nothing diminishes an Italian dish more than mushy pasta. So follow the directions on the box, pay attention to cooking time, and test a bite to check when the pasta is almost done. Italians love their pasta "al dente," which means firm enough to chew, even to the point of still having a firm core at the center. Most Americans like their pasta a bit softer, but try not

to extend your cooking time more than one minute past al dente – and experiment to learn to appreciate the texture of pasta that is cooked just right.

9. **Make a big batch as long as you are cooking** – When you find a recipe you like, don't be shy about doubling down on the quantity. As many recipes suggest, you can freeze half before cooking to make an equally delicious meal next week or month. Or you can just save the leftovers for later in the week. In many cases, the flavor of leftovers improves.

10. **Make sure to select a male eggplant** – Don't laugh, everyone in Sant' Arsenio takes this distinction seriously, because female eggplants have more seeds and are therefore more bitter. You can determine an eggplant's gender by inspecting its "bellybutton." Female eggplant bellybuttons tend to be linear slits, while male's are circular. This tip alone makes this book a bargain!

Other Basic Items Every Kitchen Needs

- Chicken Broth
- Eggs
- Potatoes
- All purpose flour
- Non-stick spray such as Pam
- Salt, black pepper, and white pepper
- Oregano, basil, and parsley
- Balsamic vinegar for salads
- Vegetable oil
- White vinegar for cooking and marinating
- Italian Bread

ANTIPASTI

CAPONATINA PAISANO

This eggplant appetizer recipe is served cold, so you can make it in advance.

½ cup olive oil
2 male eggplants (see page 7), peeled and cut in 1-inch pieces
1 cup celery, sliced in ½-inch pieces
1 large onion, sliced and chopped
2 cups tomato sauce (see page 17)
1 cup water
½ jar green olives cut in half
½ jar capers (optional)
1 heaping teaspoon sugar
¼ cup red wine vinegar

1. Add eggplant to heated olive oil, fry until brown (about 5 minutes) and remove.
2. Sauté celery and onions for 5 minutes and remove.
3. Heat tomato sauce and water for 5 minutes over medium heat and then add olives, capers (optional), eggplant, celery and onions, and vinegar.
4. Add salt, sugar, and crushed red pepper to taste.
5. Cook 6-7 minutes longer over medium heat.
6. Serve cold as an appetizer.

GRANDMA'S DEVILED EGGS

Grandma invented this recipe, which is a family favorite. According to Grandma, roasting fresh red pepper yourself over an open flame adds much more flavor using canned pimento.

6 eggs
1 tablespoon white vinegar
2 tablespoons mayonnaise
Roast pepper (pimento) sliced thin

1. Boil eggs 10 minutes (until good and hard), allow to cool, and peel the shells.
2. Cut the eggs in half, remove the yolks and crush the yolks well.
3. Mix vinegar, salt and pepper with egg yolks and add enough mayonnaise for soft paste.
4. Fill the eggs and garnish with roasted pepper (pimento).

PICKLED EGGPLANT ALA CARLA

If you invest 20 minutes in the summer when eggplants are in season, you can enjoy this appetizer all year. These are ready to eat in one week, but flavor improves with time. Refrigerate after opening and use all year.

1 large male eggplant (see page 7)
2 cups white vinegar
1 teaspoon salt

1. Peel the eggplant and slice into strips smaller than the size of your little finger.
2. Put in glass jar and cover with white vinegar.
3. Add salt and seal well.
4. When serving, put a little olive oil and minced garlic on top.

PICKLED GREEN TOMATOES

When your tomato plants are peaking, pick some when they are still green to enjoy for the rest of the year. These are ready to eat after one week, but flavor improves with time. Refrigerate after opening.

6-8 green tomatoes (more if they are small)
2 cups white vinegar
1 teaspoon salt

1. Wash tomatoes and slice into halves, quarters or eighths depending on size.
2. Put in glass jar, cover with white vinegar, add salt and seal well.
3. Serve cold, putting a little olive oil and minced garlic on top.

Frese ala Flora

This classic recipe from Sant' Arsenio makes delicious hard wheat biscuits

3 cups whole wheat flour
1 cup white flour
½ cup vegetable oil
1 envelope dry yeast
1 teaspoon salt

1. Preheat oven to 375° F.
2. Mix yeast with luke warm water and wait five minutes
3. Mix all ingredients in mixing bowl, with mixer or by hand with spoon.
4. Knead the dough on a hard surface sprinkled with flour, cover and let rise 2 hours.
5. Break dough into quarters, roll each into a "tube" about 10 inches long, place on oiled cookie sheet and let rise 1 hour.
6. Cut into 2-inch segments with knife and bake 30 minutes at 375°.
7. Remove from oven, cut pieces with serated knife about ½ inch, and lay pieces flat.
8. Bake 15 minutes more at 375° F.

MARINATED MUSHROOMS CARMELINA

With these mushrooms in your refrigerator, you'll have a zesty appetizer to spice up any meal.

3 pounds fresh mushrooms (mixed varieties, if possible)
1 teaspoon salt
1 quart water
1 quart white vinegar
1 quart canola oil (or vegetable oil)

1. Mix water, vinegar and salt and bring to a boil.
2. Add mushrooms and boil for 2-3 minutes.
3. Spread mushrooms on paper towel and let dry overnight.
4. Store mushrooms in canola oil in a sealed jar.
5. Serve with a little minced garlic on top (optional).
6. Refrigerate after opening.

STUFFED MUSHROOMS SAN RUFO

This was a holiday favorite in Sant' Arsenio, made with the best mushrooms, which came from the neighboring village of San Rufo. Note that you should not soak mushrooms in water to wash them; just brush them off with a paper towel.

1 small box of large mushrooms
1 cup Italian breadcrumbs
1 small tube of anchovy paste (½ small can of anchovies mashed up)
2 tablespoons butter or margarine
3 tablespoons olive oil
¼ teaspoon salt
white pepper

1. Preheat oven to 350° F.
2. Cut off mushroom stems, chop them finely, and sauté the chopped stems in butter.
3. Mix in breadcrumbs, anchovy paste, salt, and pepper.
4. Add enough olive oil for the consistency of peanut butter.
5. Stuff the mushroom caps with this paste.
6. Bake for 15 minutes on a cookie sheet sprayed with Pam.

STUFFED PEPPERS SANT' ARSENIO

This dish was a staple in Sant' Arsenio in the days when families depended on their gardens for most of the food.

2 large peppers
(green, red or yellow – or a combination)
1 cup mushrooms
1 cup Italian breadcrumbs
1 small tube of anchovy paste (or half of a small can of anchovies mashed up)
2 tablespoons butter or margarine
3 tablespoons olive oil
Salt and white pepper to taste

1. Preheat oven to 350° F.
2. Cut peppers in quarters and remove the seeds and insides.
3. Chop up mushrooms finely with knife and sauté in butter (only 1-2 minutes).
4. Mix mushrooms with bread crumbs, anchovy paste, white pepper and salt to taste.
5. Add enough olive oil for a consistency of peanut butter.
6. Fill the peppers with this mixture.
7. Bake for 20 minutes on a cookie sheet sprayed with Pam.

SAUCES

FIORI DI ZUCCHINI SAUCE

Whenever you find zucchini flowers at the grocery story, grab them. Even better, grow your own zucchini in your garden. Pick the blossoms in the morning when they are fully opened.

Large bowl of zucchini blossoms
4 tablespoons olive oil
1 tablespoon minced garlic
1 cup tomato sauce

1. Wash and chop zucchini blossoms into ½ inch pieces.
2. Sauté garlic in olive oil in deep saucepan.
3. Add tomato sauce and heat 5 minutes.
4. Add zucchini blossoms and crushed red pepper to taste.
5. Serve over pasta cooked al dente – spaghetti pasta works best.

FLORA'S PESTO SAUCE

This pesto sauce is fast, healthy, and you don't even need to turn on the heat – except to boil the pasta. Short pasta works best, such as bowls or shells.

1 pound pasta
2 cups fresh basil leaves with stems removed
½ cup pignoli nuts (pine nuts)
2 tablespoons minced garlic
4 tablespoons olive oil
2 tablespoons parmesan/romano cheese
Salt and crushed red pepper to taste

1. Finely chop basil leaves and pine nuts.
2. Mix in garlic, olive oil, and parmesan/romano cheese, salt and pepper.
3. Add more oil and cheese if you like.
4. Serve over hot pasta cooked al dente.

GRANDMA'S MARINARA SAUCE

Marinara sauce is used for making pizzaiola dishes, such as Pop's Pork Pizzaiola. Always make extra Marinara sauce to keep in the fridge or freezer so that you can make a gourmet dish on Thursday night in just 10 minutes.

1 large can (102 oz.) of diced tomatoes and tomato juice
6 tablespoons olive oil
2 tablespoons minced garlic
Salt and crushed red pepper to taste

1. Sauté minced garlic in olive oil.
2. Add diced tomatoes, salt and red pepper to taste.
3. Cook over medium heat 20 minutes.

MARCO'S REMARKABLE TUNA SAUCE

Pop took great pride in inventing this dish, which is a family favorite. It's quick, easy, healthy, delicious – and only 58 cents a serving, according to Pop.

1 cup tomato sauce
2 small cans or 1 large can of chunk tuna in water (dark tuna has more flavor)
4 tablespoons olive oil
1 tablespoon minced garlic
Salt, crushed red pepper, and oregano to taste

1. Sauté minced garlic in oil in a deep frying pan.
2. Add tuna and sauté 2-3 minutes.
3. Add tomato sauce, hot pepper, and oregano and simmer 2-3 minutes.
4. Add 1 cup water and a pinch of salt.
5. Cover and simmer 10 minutes to get the flavors to mix.
6. Serve with pasta cooked al dente – spaghetti works best – and parmesan/romano cheese.

GRANDMA'S TOMATO SAUCE

This is one of the core ingredients in Grandma's cooking system, so you should always have tomato sauce on hand in the fridge, with a backup supply in the freezer. Make a big batch and save in one-pint plastic containers with screw-on tops. When you run out of tomato sauce, it's time to make another big batch!

1 large can crushed tomatoes (102 oz.)
1 large onion
3 stalks celery, chopped
3-4 carrots, very finely chopped
10 tablespoons olive oil
1 tablespoon basil/parsley mix
1 tablespoon minced garlic
6 ounces beef, pork, or sausage cut up in small pieces (optional for additional flavor)
Salt and crushed red pepper to taste

1. Sauté onions and garlic in olive oil until shiny (5-6 minutes over low heat).
2. Add celery and carrots and sauté 3-4 more minutes, stirring frequently.
3. Optional: Add beef, pork or sausage (not chicken) cut in small pieces and cook until the liquid evaporates.
4. Add crushed tomatoes and stir.
5. Add salt (about ½ teaspoon) and red pepper (4-5 good shakes) to taste.
6. Bring to boil and then simmer on low heat for 45 minutes.
7. Add parsley/basil mix and stir just before serving.

MUSHROOM SAUCE ALA MAMMA

This mushroom sauce, which is a staple throughout southern Italy, takes only 10 minutes (if you have tomato sauce already made) and melts in your mouth.

1 box of mushrooms, sliced
1 stick of butter
1 cup tomato sauce
White pepper

1. Melt the butter in a pan.
2. Sauté mushrooms 5 minutes.
3. Add tomato sauce and cook over medium heat 5 minutes.
4. Add pepper to taste and serve over pasta.

POP'S BOLOGNESE SAUCE

This recipe was one of Marco's specialities. With a green salad, a dish of pasta with Pop's Bolognese Sauce makes a complete meal. Make a double batch to enjoy leftovers later in the week.

1 pound ground meat (hamburger)
1 large onion, chopped very finely
4 tablespoons olive oil
1 tablespoon basil/parsley mix
1 15-ounce can crushed tomatoes
1 pound pasta
Salt and crushed red pepper to taste

1. Sauté onion in olive oil until golden.
2. Add meat and cook until the liquid is absorbed/evaporated (about 15 minutes).
3. Add crushed tomatoes, salt, crushed red pepper, and basil/parsley mix.
4. Reduce heat and cook for 20 minutes.
5. Serve over pasta cooked al dente – short pasta works best, such as ziti, small wheels, etc.

CLAM SAUCE CATERINA

If your tomato sauce and minced garlic are already made, clam sauce only takes 5 minutes. The secret is not to over-cook the clams, which makes them tough.

1 cup clams, chopped finely
2 cups tomato sauce
4 tablespoons olive oil
1 tablespoon minced garlic
Fresh parsley – or 1
tablespoon parsley/basil mix

1. Chop the clams finely.
2. Sauté garlic in olive oil.
3. Add clams and stir for only one minute
4. Add salt and pepper and parsley to taste.
5. Add tomato sauce and serve over pasta as soon as hot

SHRIMP SAUCE SALERNO

If your tomato sauce and minced garlic are already made, this shrimp sauce only takes 5 minutes. The secret is not to over-cook the shrimp, which makes them tough.

1 cup small shrimp
2 cups tomato sauce
4 tablespoons olive oil
1 tablespoon minced garlic
Fresh parsley – or 1
tablespoon parsley/basil mix

1. Sauté garlic in olive oil.
2. Add shrimp and stir for only 1-2 minutes, no more.
3. Add salt and crushed red pepper – and parsley! – to taste.
4. Add tomato sauce and serve as soon as hot over pasta cooked al dente.

PASTA

Fettuccine ala Franca

This makes a wonderful white sauce with peas and pasta that is indescribably good – in less than 10 minutes.

1 stick butter
1 can green peas (or frozen peas)
1 cup heavy cream
1 package of fettuccine pasta
Salt and white pepper
2 tablespoons grated parmesan/romano cheese

1. Boil fettuccine pasta al dente.
2. Melt butter in large pan.
3. Sauté peas for 3 minutes.
4. Add heavy cream and cook over low heat 5 minutes.
5. Add fettucine to the sauce and mix.
6. Add grated cheese and salt and pepper to taste, mix and serve.

Pasta Orzo ala Flora

This pasta dish is a traditional favorite from Sant' Arsenio and can be served as either as the main dish or a side course.

½ cup pancetta cubes (fresh salt pork, not smoked)
6 scallions cut in 1-inch pieces (or onions or shallots)
1 pound frozen green peas
1 cup chicken broth
4 tablespoons olive oil
1 tablespoon minced garlic

1. Boil 1 cup orzo with salt 15 minutes, drain and set aside.
2. Sauté garlic in olive oil.
3. Add pancetta, scallions and crushed red pepper and cook 5 minutes over medium heat.
4. Add green peas and cook 10 more minutes.
5. Add chicken broth and cook 5 more minutes.
6. Add the cooked orzo and mix.

FLORA'S FRITATTA DI PASTA

When you have cooked pasta left over, don't throw it out. You are ready to make Frittata di Pasta (Spaghetti Pie), a staple in S'ant Arsenio. You can use any kind of spaghetti, but thin spaghetti (capellini) works best.

4-5 large eggs
½ cup milk
¼ pound mozzarella cheese, cut in small pieces
½ pound cooked spaghetti
1 tablespoon olive oil
White pepper

1. Beat 4-5 eggs with milk, add mozzarella cheese and cooked spaghetti.
2. Add salt and white pepper (black pepper makes the frittatta too dark).
3. Oil a frying pan, heat it and when hot, put in spaghetti-egg mixture.
4. Cook over medium-high for 2-3 minutes to brown, then lower heat and cook 15 minutes. (If your frying pan can go into the oven, you can bake at 350 for 15 minutes after browning).
5. Cut into wedges like a pie and serve hot.

Grandma's Pasta with Lentils

This is another staple of southern Italy. With lentils, always sauté onions instead of garlic.

1 pound bag of dry lentils
1 large onion, chopped and sliced
2 stalks celery, chopped
5 tablespoons tomato sauce (see page 17)

1. Add lentils and celery to 8 cups hot water, cover and cook until tender, 30-40 minutes.
2. Chop and slice one large onion and sauté in large saucepan 6-7 minutes until golden.
3. Add the cooked lentils and tomato sauce and cook at medium heat for 5 minutes.
4. Add salt and crushed red pepper to taste.
5. Serve in bowl over very small pasta, such as ditalini or elbow pasta.

Pasta con Escarole di Sala Consalina

This delicious and healthy dish takes just 15 minutes to make.

1 pound of escarole washed and cut in 3-inch pieces
4 tablespoons olive oil
1 teaspoon minced garlic
¼ cup water
Salt and crushed red pepper

1. Sauté garlic olive oil.
2. Add water, escarole, and salt and pepper to taste.
3. Cover the pot and cook over medium heat 7-8 minutes, stirring occasionally and adding water if needed so as not to burn.
4. Serve over short pasta of your choice, such as ziti, rotini, or mettazani.

HOMEMADE RAVIOLI ALA NENETTA

Making homemade ravioli on Thanksgiving morning is a family tradition and a wonderful group project for the grandkids.

Ingredients for Dough

1 pound flour
2 eggs beaten
¼ tablespoons salt
¼ cup warm water,
enough to make soft
dough

Ingredients for Filling

2 pounds ricotta cheese
2 tablespoons chopped
parsley
4 eggs, beaten
½ cup parmesan cheese
Salt and pepper to taste

1. Mix the ingredients for the dough, knead the dough, cover and let stand 30 minutes.
2. Then cut dough in quarters and roll each piece with rolling pin about 1/8" thick.
3. Put a heaping tablespoon of ricotta mix 4" down from top edge of the dough and 3" apart.
4. Fold the dough over this row of cheese dabs and cut between each with knife in 3" squares.
5. Use a fork to press and seal the edges (the kids love to do this).
6. Place 6-8 at a time in a deep pot of boiling water and cook for about 3 minutes (about one minute after they float to the surface).
7. Serve with tomato sauce (see page 17) and parmesan/romano cheese.

Lasagna ala Marilena

This lasagna recipe is foolproof and easy to make, since there is no need to boil the lasagna first! This recipe has been modified from the original recipe from Sant' Arsenio. For vegetarian lasagna, simply substitute chopped, uncooked spinach for the meat layer and use vegetarian tomato sauce.

1 box (9 ounces) Barilla *No Boil* Lasagna, uncooked

2 eggs

1 container (15 ounces) ricotta cheese

4 cups shredded mozzarella cheese (divided)

½ cup grated parmesan cheese

2 tablespoons parsley chopped

1 pound ground beef or sausage

4 ½ cups of tomato sauce (see page 17)

Salt and pepper to taste

1. Preheat oven to 375° F.
2. In medium bowl, beat eggs, ricotta, parsley, 2 cups mozzarella cheese, parmesan cheese and salt and pepper to taste (start with 1 teaspoon each), and set this mixture aside.
3. In a 13 x 9 x 3 pan, spread 1 cup of sauce on bottom of pan.
4. Layer in the following order: 4 uncooked lasagna noodles (they will overlap), 1/3 of the ricotta cheese mixture, half the browned meat, 1 cup mozzarella cheese, and 1 cup sauce.
5. Next layer: 4 uncooked lasagna noodles, 1/3 part of the ricotta cheese mixture, and 1 ½ cups sauce.
6. Next layer: 4 uncooked lasagna noodles, remaining ricotta mixture and remained meat, 1 cup of sauce.
7. For top layer: 4 uncooked lasagna noodles, remaining sauce, and remaining 1 cup mozzarella.
8. Bake covered with foil for 50-60 minutes.
9. Uncover and continue cooking until all the cheese is melted on the top (about 5 minutes).
10. Let stand 15 minutes before serving. NOTE: If you are using a more shallow pan, such as a 13 x 9 x 2, just make 3 layers to avoid boiling over.

PASTA AL FORNO CAMPANIA

The pasta in this dish, which come from the region of Italy called Campania, is first boiled and then baked. The flavors are wonderful, and the leftovers are even better.

1 box penne pasta
½ cup shredded mozzarella cheese
½ cup parmesan cheese
15 ounces ricotta cheese
2 eggs
4 cups tomato sauce (see page 17)
3 tablespoons chopped fresh parsley – or 1 tablespoon dry parsley

1. Preheat oven to 350° F.
2. Cook pasta al dente and let cool.
3. Mix ricotta, parmesan, eggs, parsley and add salt and black pepper.
4. Layer bottom of large baking dish with 1/3 of the tomato sauce.
5. Add layers of half the pasta, half the ricotta mix, and 1/3 tomato sauce.
6. Add more layers of the remaining pasta, ricotta mix, and sauce.
7. Add mozzarella cheese on top.
8. Bake 45 minutes.

PRESTO PASTA WITH PEAS

No pasta dish is faster than this one. You can make this dish – and have plenty of time to make a salad – in the time it takes for the water to boil and the pasta to cook.

1 16-ounce can of green peas
1 large onion, chopped
4 tablespoons tomato sauce (see page 17)

1. Sauté onion in olive oil until golden.
2. Add tomato sauce, salt and crushed red pepper to taste.
3. Stir quickly and add a can of green peas.
4. Serve over pasta cooked al dente – short pasta works best – shells, elbows, twists, etc.

Pasta e Fagioli Paisano

This dish is a staple across southern Italy. You can use any variety of beans, but according to Grandma red beans have the most flavor. Of course, you can make this with fresh beans, but canned beans make it much faster. Use very small pasta, such as elbows or ditalini.

2 cans of either white, red, or black beans
4 tablespoons olive oil
1 heaping tablespoon minced garlic
4 tablespoons tomato sauce (see page 17)
Crushed red pepper to taste

1. Drain the liquid from the canned beans and rinse with water.
2. Sauté garlic in olive oil.
3. Add the beans and tomato sauce and cook 20 minutes over medium heat.
4. Add crushed red pepper to taste just before serving.
5. Cook the pasta al dente and drain.
6. Mix the pasta into the beans and still 2 minutes before serving to soak up flavor.

GINGER'S PASTA WITH RAPINI

If you haven't discovered rapini, it's time to. This dark green vegetable is kind of a cross between broccoli and spinach. It's a little bitter but just delicious sautéed with garlic. Most grocery stores only have rapini periodically, so keep an eye out for this delicacy.

1 large bunch of rapini
4 tablespoons olive oil
1 tablespoon minced garlic
½ cup water
Crushed red pepper
Salt and pepper

1. Wash rapini and trim and throw away the stems.
2. Sauté garlic and crushed red pepper in olive oil in deep saucepan.
3. Add rapini. Salt and pepper to taste.
4. Toss the rapini in the olive oil for 30 seconds or so.
5. Add ½ cup of water and cover the dish, cooking over medium heat.
6. Cook until tender, 5 -7 minutes – don't cook it too long or it becomes bitter.
7. Serve over pasta – rigatoni or ziti work best.

Polpitte di Riso Straordinarie

Grandma's rice balls are always a big hit at holiday parties. They are even better as leftovers.

One pound bag of long grain white rice
6 large eggs
2 pound container of ricotta cheese
1 pound shredded mozzarella
½ cup grated parmesan cheese
2½ cups tomato sauce (see page 17)
Salt and white pepper

1. Preheat oven to 350° F.
2. Cook rice al dente, rinse in cold water and let cool.
3. Mix eggs, ricotta, mozzarella and parmesan cheese in a large bowl with salt and pepper to taste.
4. Add this to the cooled rice, mix, and roll into balls about the size golf balls.
5. Spread tomato sauce in a large rectangular baking dish about ¼ inch deep and then place rice balls with a little room in between.
6. Add the rest of the tomato sauce on top.
7. Bake for 15 minutes covered with foil and then 15 more minutes uncovered.

PASTA FAGIOLI ALA GINGER

This is the easiest and most satisfying dish on a cold day. Plus it takes no thought ahead of time as you probably have all the ingredients in the house already.

1 tablespoon minced garlic
2 tablespoons of olive oil
1-2 fresh tomatoes chopped or ½ can whole tomatoes chopped up
1 can chicken broth
1 can white beans – cannellini are best – drained and rinsed
1 bunch fresh greens – escarole, kale, or spinach
½ pound cooked pasta - small shells, ditalini, or break up some spaghetti
Salt and pepper

1. Sauté garlic in olive oil for 1-2 minutes in a soup pot.
2. Add crushed pepper to olive oil after 1 minute.
3. Add chopped tomatoes to oil and stir for about a minute.
4. Add a can of broth and a can of water to the pot.
5. Bring liquid to a boil and add fresh green vegetables.
6. Lower heat and simmer while the pasta in cooking in another pot.
7. Add rinsed beans to broth and simmer for 2 minutes just to get the beans and soup hot.
8. Remove soup from the heat and stir in pasta. Salt and pepper to taste.

VEGETABLES

ASPARAGUS ARROSTITO

If you like asparagus, you will love this recipe for broiled asparagus.

1 big bunch of fresh
asparagus
1/2 cup breadcrumbs
3 tablespoons grated
cheese
1 tablespoons chopped
parsley
1 tablespoons minced garlic
1 tablespoons olive oil

1. Boil the asparagus for 5-6 minutes to cook partially.
2. Spread asparagus in large baking pan/cookie sheet one layer deep.
3. Mix remaining ingredients with enough olive oil to moisten the crumbs.
4. Sprinkle the crumb mix on top of the aspargus.
5. Broil in middle of oven until breadcrumbs are crisp (about 6-8 minutes). Don't burn!

BROCCOLI DI BUONABITACOLO

Garlic and red pepper transform plain old broccoli into a dish to re-member. Keep adding a little more red pepper each time you make this dish, until your family and friends begin to whimper. Buonabita-colo is a small town in Campania, the name of which literally trans-lates to "a good place to live."

1 pound of broccoli, cut up
with heavy stems removed
4 tablespoons olive oil
1 tablespoon minced garlic
½ cup water
Salt and crushed red pepper

1. In deep saucepan, sauté garlic in olive oil.
2. Add broccoli, water, salt and crushed red pepper to taste (at least 2-3 good shakes).
3. Cover, simmer over low heat, stirring occasionally for about 15 minutes until tender.

CIAMBOTA DI SANT' ARSENIO (EVERYTHING TOGETHER)

This vegetable medley relies on the motto of the village of S'ant Arsenio, "The more you put in the pot, the more you will have for dinner." The ingredients are all natural. The secret is adding the vegetables in the right order, because some require more time to cook than others.

6 tablespoons olive oil
1 medium onion
1 large potato
1 red pepper
1 green pepper
3 celery stalks
½ small male eggplant
(see page 7)
2 peeled carrots
2 small zucchini
2 fresh tomatoes
2 cups mushrooms
Salt and crushed red pepper

1. Cut all the vegetables by hand in small pieces.
2. Sauté sliced onion in olive oil and add the other vegetables, cut in bite-size pieces in the order listed: 1) potato, 2) peppers, 3) celery, 4) eggplant, 5) carrots, 6) zucchini, 7) tomatoes, 8) mushrooms.
3. Add salt and red pepper to taste.
4. Continue to stir as you add vegetables for 15 minutes total cooking time.

SAUTÉED PEPPERS AND ONIONS ALA LUIGI

This is a versatile side dish as well a terrific addition to grilled Italian sausage.

2 large onions
2 large peppers – green, red or yellow or a combination
4 tablespoons olive oil
Salt and crushed red pepper

1. Slice onions into 1½-inch strips about ¼ inch wide.
2. Sauté onions in olive oil 6-7 minutes until golden.
3. Add sliced peppers and sauté until tender, about 5 more minutes.
4. Add salt and red pepper to taste.

DANDELIONS ALA MARCO

Pop taught us that dandelions are more than a weed. In fact, dandelion leaves are healthy and delicious when sautéed with garlic. Pick tender sprouts in the springtime or after a rain so the leaves are not too bitter – in a place that is free of pesticides and away from dogs. These can be mixed raw into a green salad to add zip or cooked below as a side dish.

Large bunch of green
dandelion leaves
4 tablespoons olive oil
1 tablespoon minced garlic
½ cup water

1. Wash dandelion leaves well.
2. Sauté garlic in olive oil in deep saucepan.
3. Add dandelions and sauté 3 minutes.
4. Add water, cook until tender (about10-15 minutes), and test a stem to check that it's done.
5. Add salt and crushed red pepper to taste.

EGGPLANT NINO

This eggplant dish is quick, easy, and simply melts in your mouth. Check Tip #10 to learn how to identify a male eggplant, which is more tender than a female because it has fewer seeds.

1 male eggplant (see page 7)
2 eggs, beaten
2 cups Italian breadcrumbs
2 tablespoons chopped
fresh basil
2 cups olive oil
1 pound mozzarella cheese

1. Preheat oven to 350° F.
2. Slice large eggplant crosswise in ½" round slices.
3. Mix breadcrumbs and chopped basil.
4. Dip eggplant pieces in beaten eggs and then in breadcrumb mix.
5. Deep fry in olive oil 1 minute per side until breadcrumbs are golden.
6. Add sliced mozzarella cheese on top.
7. Bake 5 minutes at 350° F. until the cheese melts.

FIORI DI ZUCCHINI ITALIANA

Zucchini blossoms are food of the Gods. Keep an eye out in the spring for this seasonal delicacy at your grocery store. Even better, grow your own zucchini in your garden. Pick the blossoms in the morning when they are fully opened. To make these even more delicious, stuff the blossoms with ricotta or mozzarella cheese and deep fry.

Large bowl of zucchini blossoms
½ cup flour
½ teaspoon baking powder
¼ teaspoon garlic salt
1 egg
½ cup milk
1 tablespoon vegetable oil

1. Mix flour, baking powder, and garlic salt.
2. Beat egg with oil and milk.
3. Combine the above ingredients and mix into batter.
4. Dip the whole zucchini blossoms in the batter.
5. Fry on hot skillet with vegetable oil 1-2 minutes on a side, turning once.

GREEN BEANS GIGI

This recipe makes green beans a treat. The tomato sauce tenderizes the beans, while the garlic and red pepper add some zip.

1 pound of green beans with stems removed
1 medium onion
1 tablespoon olive oil
½ tablespoon minced garlic
1 cup tomato sauce (see page 17)
Salt and crushed red pepper

1. Chop onion in 1-inch pieces and sauté in olive oil until golden.
2. Add minced garlic and sauté 2 minutes.
3. Add green beans and stir to coat with oil.
4. Add salt and crushed red pepper to taste.
5. Add tomato sauce and simmer about 10 minutes until tender.

Escarole and Bean Soup Donato

Most people think of escarole as a kind of lettuce for making salad. This simple dish brings out escarole's wonderful flavor and texture when cooked. Nothing is healthier, so make this one of your staples.

2 bunches of escarole lettuce
1 can cooked beans (red beans have the most flavor)
½ cup tomato sauce (see page 17)
4 tablespoons olive oil
1 tablespoon minced garlic
6 ounces water, approximately

1. Drain and wash beans and set aside.
2. Wash escarole and cut in 1½ inch pieces.
3. Sauté minced garlie in olive oil.
4. Add escarole and sauté 1-2 minutes to coat with oil.
5. Add water, lower the heat and cook 5-6 minutes (check the stem to see when it's done).
6. Add tomato sauce and salt to taste and cook 5 more minutes over medium heat.
7. Add beans and cook 4-5 minutes, adding more water if needed.

Eggplant Rollatini Vito

This fancy eggplant dish, which was popular in Sant' Arsenio for holidays, makes for a great vegetarian main course.

1 large male eggplant (see page 7)
preferably a male eggplant
2 eggs, beaten
2 cups Italian breadcrumbs
½ cup parmesan cheese
2 tablespoons chopped basil
2 cups olive oil
1 pound mozzarella cheese
Salt and pepper

1. Preheat oven to 350° F.
2. Slice eggplant lengthwise about 2 inches wide and as thin as possible, about 1/8 inch.
3. Mix egg with salt and pepper; set aside.
4. Mix breadcrumbs and parmesan cheese in a separate dish.
5. Dip the eggplant slices in the egg mixture, then dip the slices in the breadcrumb mixture.
6. Fry slowly in a little oil 1-2 minutes a side and then let cool on paper towels.
7. Roll up each slice around a piece of mozzarella cheese and basil.
8. Bake for 30 minutes – or bake in a pan with tomato sauce and parmesan cheese.

Piselli ala Nonna Maria

This dish, featuring green peas, was a favorite of Marco's mother, Maria, because it is so fast and easy to make.

3 tablespoons olive oil
1 can green peas (or package of frozen peas)
1 onions sliced
1 teaspoon oregano
Salt and black pepper

1. Coat the bottom of a large pan with olive oil.
2. Sauté onions until cooked.
3. Add peas, oregano, salt and pepper to taste.
4. Cook at medium heat for 3-4 minutes.

KALE CON SPEZZIE

The somewhat bitter taste of kale turns off some people, especially children. However, when kale is sautéed in garlic, it's as delicious as it is healthy for you.

1 pound kale, torn in pieces
4 tablespoons olive oil
1 tablespoon minced garlic
½ cup water
Salt and crushed red pepper

1. In deep saucepan, sauté garlic in olive oil.
2. Add kale, water, salt to taste and at least 2-3 shakes of crushed red pepper.
3. Cover, simmer over low heat, stirring occasionally for about 20 minutes.
4. Add more water if necessary. Check the stems to see when it's cooked.

PIZZA DI PATATE SISELLA

This potato pie, was a favorite of Grandma's sister Sisella, has been perfected over generations in Sant' Arsenio. Melts in your mouth and is great for leftovers.

1 dozen medium potatoes
6 large eggs
1 cup grated parmesan or romano cheese
4 ounces mozzarella cheese cut very small
1 teaspoon salt
½ teaspoon white pepper
½ cup Italian breadcrumbs

1. Preheat oven to 350° F.
2. Peel one dozen medium potatoes, boil until tender, mash very fine.
3. Mix with eggs, grated cheese, and mozzarella cheese for a creamy mix.
4. Add salt and white pepper to taste.
5. Pour into a glass baking dish sprayed with Pam.
6. Sprinkle breadcrumbs on top.
7. Bake for 30 minutes.

PATATE ARROSTITE MARILENA

This potato side dish goes great with beef, chicken, pork or seafood. The crispier the better. Make plenty because the leftovers are great.

8 medium potatoes
5 tablespoons olive oil
1 ½ tablespoons oregano
Salt and black pepper

1. Preheat oven to 400° F.
2. Wash potatoes and cut into wedges.
3. Spray glass baking dish with Pam, add olive oil and potatoes, and turn to coat.
4. Sprinkle generously with oregano, and salt and pepper to taste.
5. Bake 30-40 minutes until tender, turning twice – and a little longer for crispy.

VALLO DI DIANO WEDDING SOUP

This dish gets its name from the bride's veil created by adding the egg and parmesan mixture at the end. Just add vegetables that are in season – carrots, celery, onions, parsley.

3 quarts chicken broth
½ cup grated parmesan cheese
1 bunch escarole cut in 1-inch pieces (remove outer leaves and stems)
Vegetables of your choice
30 small meatballs (equivalent of one pound, see page 52)
3 eggs
½ bunch chopped parsley

1. Heat chicken broth in a big pot.
2. Add escarole and (frozen) meatballs.
3. Cook 15-20 minutes at medium heat.
4. Salt and pepper to taste.
5. Pour eggs beaten with grated cheese slowly into boiling soup to make the veil.

ZUCCHINI ALA NENETTA

Grandma learned this delicious dish from her grandmother, Maria.

1 pound zucchini diced in 1-inch cubes
4 tablespoons olive oil
1 teaspoon garlic
½ cup tomato sauce (see page 17)
2 eggs beaten
2 tablespoons grated parmesan/romano cheese
2 tablespoons Italian breadcrumbs
1 teaspoon water

1. Beat the eggs and add cheese, breadcrumbs, salt and pepper to taste, and add water if necessary for a soft paste consistency then set aside.
2. Sauté garlic in olive oil.
3. Add zucchini and cook over medium heat 20 minutes.
4. Add tomato sauce and cook 5 minutes.
5. With a teaspoon drop dabs of the egg mixture on top of zucchini.
6. Cover and cook low for 2 minutes.

ZUCCHINI E PATATE
ALA NONNA MADDALENA

This vegetable dish was a favorite of Nenetta's mother, Maddalena.

4 medium potatoes, cubed
2 medium zucchini, cubed
2 medium onions, sliced
3 fresh plum tomatoes, sliced
3 tablespoons olive oil
½ teaspoon crushed red pepper
4-5 leaves fresh basil, coarsely chopped
Salt and black pepper

1. Coat the bottom of a large pan with olive oil and heat to medium.
2. Sauté crushed red pepper 1 minute.
3. Add onions and sauté 3 minutes until partially cooked.
4. Add tomatoes and sauté 2 more minutes.
5. Add potatoes and cook 5 minutes over medium heat.
6. Add zucchini, basil, salt & pepper.
7. Cover and cook 10 minutes.
8. Garnish with romano cheese.

CHICKEN

CHICKEN CACCIATORE SEBASTIANO

According to the lore of Sant' Arsenio, chicken cacciatore is the "dish of the hunter," the recipe originally developed for quail and other sport birds. This tender and tasty chicken dish can either be eaten as a stand-alone dish or served over pasta.

1 pound chicken pieces, either thighs, breasts or both
1 container fresh mushrooms, about 2 cups
1 large onion, chopped
4 tablespoons olive oil
1 quart can of crushed tomatoes
½ cup water
½ cup white wine
½ tablespoon salt
Crushed red pepper
Oregano

1. Clean chicken and cut up in about 2-inch pieces.
2. Wash and slice mushrooms.
3. Sauté onion in olive oil until golden.
4. Add chicken and cook covered on low heat until the liquid evaporates, about 20 minutes.
5. Add ½ cup water and continue cooking until liquid evaporates, about 20 minutes.
6. Add white wine, tomatoes and mushrooms.
7. Add salt, three shakes of crushed red pepper, and a pinch of oregano.
8. Reduce heat to low and cook for 20 minutes.

CHICKEN CARDINALE COIRO

All the ingredients are from the old country, but Uncle Tony perfected this dish in his restaurant on Long Island.

2 chicken breasts
1 cup flour
¼ cup vegetable oil
2 tablespoon butter
2 slices prosciutto
1 ounce pimento
4 tablespoons white wine
½ cup chicken broth
4 ounces mozzarella cheese

1. Filet chicken breasts in 1/4-inch slices.
2. Roll chicken filets in flour.
3. Sauté chicken in vegetable oil in hot pan 1 minute per side.
4. Drain oil and add 2 tablespoons butter.
5. Place prosciutto and pimento on top of each piece.
6. Add white wine and chicken broth.
7. Place a piece of mozzarella cheese on top of each piece.
8. Cover and simmer about 3 minutes until cheese melts.

CHICKEN PIZZAIOLA SALA CONSALINA

This chicken dish melts in your mouth because the marinara sauce tenderizes the chicken. Make plenty because it's even better as leftovers.

1 pound chicken pieces, either thighs or breasts
1 cup marinara sauce (see page 16)
4 tablespoons olive oil
1 tablespoon minced garlic
2 cups mushrooms
Salt and pepper

1. Wash chicken and cut in large pieces (cut breasts in half, use small thighs whole).
2. Sauté garlic in olive oil.
3. Add chicken pieces and braise for 2 minutes.
4. Add marinara sauce and cook over medium heat 15 minutes.
5. Add cut up mushrooms and cook additional 10 minutes.

Chicken Marsala Vezo

Mushrooms, salami, butter, chicken broth, and Marsala wine combine to make a magical sauce.

2 chicken breasts
3 tablespoons vegetable oil
4 slices salami cut in
1/8-inch slices
1 pound mushrooms
sliced
5 tablespoons butter
2 tablespoons Marsala
wine
½ cup chicken broth
Salt and pepper

1. Sauté mushrooms in 3 tablespoons butter.
2. Filet chicken breasts in ¼-inch medallions.
3. Roll chicken pieces in flour, pan fry one minute per side.
4. Drain oil, add 2 tablespoons butter and salami, and mix.
5. Add sautéed mushrooms, Marsala wine, and chicken broth.
6. Salt and pepper to taste, simmer 3 minutes, and serve.

Chicken Francese Filomena

This Francese sauce is delectable. The secret is draining the oil after pan frying the chicken, and then using butter to create the sauce.

2 chicken breasts
1 cup flour
1 egg beaten
3 tablespoons vegetable
oil
3 tablespoons butter
¼ cup white wine
½ cup chicken broth
Lemon juice (one lemon)
Salt and pepper

1. Filet chicken breasts into medallions about ¼-inch thick.
2. Dip in egg and then dredge in flour.
3. Pan fry in hot pan with vegetable oil, one minute per side.
4. Drain oil, add butter, wine, lemon juice, and chicken broth over chicken.
5. Sprinkle in a little flour to thicken the sauce a bit.
6. Salt and pepper to taste, simmer 2-3 minutes, and serve.

CHICKEN (OR VEAL) SCALLIPINI SAPRI

Scallipini is a more fancy chicken dish. When you make scallipini, make plenty to keep in the freezer to make future meals quick and easy. Freeze the extra pieces of sautéed chicken in a freezer container, using layers of wax paper to prevent the pieces from sticking together. (Grandma suggests you reuse the wax paper that comes inside cereal boxes, which works well to separate the pieces without sticking.)

6 large chicken breasts
1 cup flour
1 cup vegetable oil
½ cup warm water with
1 chicken bullion cube
dissolved
½ cup white wine
1 cup sliced mushrooms
Salt and white pepper

1. Preheat oven to 350° F.
2. Clean the fat off several large chicken breasts and slice into large filets about ¼" thick. (Set aside the smaller pieces of chicken and freeze to have handy for other dishes.)
3. Roll the chicken slices in flour mixed with salt and pepper.
4. Sauté the chicken filets in vegetable oil over high heat until they turn white, which only takes about one minute on a side
5. Set half the filets aside for freezing for future meals.
6. Spray a large baking dish with Pam and spread out the sautéed chicken pieces in one layer.
7. Add white wine and water with a chicken bullion cube dissolved.
8. Add salt and black pepper to taste and put sliced mushrooms on top.
9. Cover with foil and bake for 30 minutes.

POLLO (OR VEAL) PARMIGIANA TEGGIANO

This is a delicious combination of two ingredients that were abundant in Sant' Arsenio, cheese and chicken, makes an elegant main course for either chicken breasts or veal.

4 chicken breasts
2 eggs
1 tablespoon milk
1 cup flour
1 cup bread crumbs
1 cup tomato sauce (see page 17)
½ cup mozzarella cheese
Salt and pepper

1. Preheat oven to 350° F.
2. Cut chicken breasts into thick slices, 2 or 3 slices per piece.
3. Spread flour in plate and coat the chicken pieces.
4. Dip the floured pieces in the eggs beaten with milk and salt and pepper.
5. Coat the chicken pieces with breadcrumbs.
6. Spread half the tomato sauce in a baking dish.
7. Put chicken pieces in dish with the rest of the tomato sauce on top.
8. Bake for 12 minutes.
9. Add mozzarella slices on top and bake for 2-3 more minutes.

CHICKEN SCARPARIELLO ANTICO

This dish was a favorite of Nenetta's mother, Maddalena. Scarpariello literally translates to "shoemaker style," a testament to the ancient roots of this dish.

1 whole chicken cut up
1 large onion sliced
1 pound mushrooms sliced
4 tablespoons olive oil
2 tablespoons minced garlic
Salt and crushed red pepper
Paprika

1. Preheat oven to 375° F.
2. Bake chicken in pan for 20 minutes (until it is about half baked).
3. Add olive oil, mushrooms, onion, garlic, salt and pepper to taste.
4. Mix all together and bake 15-20 more minutes.
5. Drain liquid, add 1 tablespoon olive oil, and toss.
6. To add color, broil for the last 5 minutes (optional).
7. Sprinkle with paprika

BEEF AND PORK

GRILLED SALSICCIA ITALIANO

Italian sausage is best when grilled and served with sautéed onions and peppers. Always select *spicy* Italian sausage; life's too short to eat *mild* sausage.

1 pound spicy Italian
sausage
4 tablespoons olive oil
1 large onion, sliced
1 pound peppers (3 red,
yellow, green peppers or a
mix)
Panini Italian bread

1. Grill the sausage over low flame 15 minutes, turning frequently.
2. Sauté onion in olive oil 3 minutes.
3. Add peppers sliced in 3-8 inch strips and sauté 10 more minutes.
4. Toast the bread and serve with the peppers and onions on top.

POP'S PORK CHOP PIZZAIOLA

Tired of pork chops that are dense and dried out. Pop knew the magic of marinara sauce, which makes the meat tender enough to eat with a fork.

1 pound pork cutlets or
pork chops
1 cup fresh mushrooms
sliced
4 tablespoons olive oil
1 tablespoon minced garlic
1 cup marinara sauce (see
page 16)
Salt and black pepper

1. Sauté garlic in olive oil in a large pan.
2. Braise pork cutlets or pork chops in the pan about 1 minute on a side.
3. Cover the pork with marinara sauce, cover, and cook 15 minutes over medium heat.
4. Add cut up mushrooms, salt and pepper to taste, cover, and cook 15 more minutes.

GRANDMA'S MEATBALLS

The secret to great meatballs is having them on hand in your freezer, ready when dinner guests arrive unexpectedly – or when you are too busy to make a trip to the grocery store. After following Grandma's recipe below, place the meatballs individually on a cookie sheet and freeze for 1-2 hours. Then place in a plastic freezer bag so that you can use as many, or as few, as you need. All you need to do is simply drop the frozen meatballs in cooking tomato sauce for 10 minutes.

2 pound chopped meat or ground pork (pork is better!)
1 cup Italian bread crumbs
1 cup milk
1 cup grated parmesan/ romano cheese
4 ounces mozzarella cheese (optional)
4 large eggs beaten
Salt and black pepper

1. Preheat oven to 350° F.
2. Soak bread crumbs in milk.
3. Mix bread crumbs with meat, cheese and eggs with a spoon or your hands and add salt and pepper to taste.
4. Mold into balls about the size of an egg.
5. Put a small piece of mozzarella or other cheese in the middle of each one (optional).
6. Bake for 5 minutes, turn once, and bake 5-6 more minutes.

MEATBALLS FOR SOUP

Follow the directions above, but mold into smaller, bite-sized meatballs of about ½-inch diameter and reduce baking time to 6-8 minutes total.

ROLLATINI RUFFIANA

This delicacy can be made with chicken breast, veal or a good cut of beef. It's well worth the time it takes to prepare.

Ingredients for mixture

1 cup grated parmesan cheese
1 pound prosciutto or salami sliced in long, thin slivers
1 tablespoon chopped parsley
1 tablespoon minced garlic
Salt and crushed red pepper

Other Ingredients

2 pounds of meat, chicken breast, veal, or beef
2 eggs
4 ounces milk
1 cup flour
¼ cup mozzarella
1 cup vegetable oil
½ cup warm water with bullion cube
½ cup white wine
2 cups fresh mushrooms

1. Preheat oven to 350° F.
2. Prepare the mixture by combining all ingredients and mixing.
3. Cut the meat in thin slices about 2 inches wide, and spread the mixture on the slices.
4. Roll the slices of meat and tie with cooking string.
5. Roll the pieces in flour.
6. Dip the pieces in the beaten eggs mixed with milk.
7. Fry in hot vegetable oil 2 minutes, turning once. (You may want to freeze half on a cookie sheet and then store in plastic freezer bag.)
8. Pour warm water with bullion and white wine into a large baking dish.
9. Place the rollatini in a pan, put the mushrooms on top, with a dot of butter on each piece.
10. Cover with foil and bake for 25-30 minutes.

SAUSAGE, PEPPERS AND ONIONS ARSENIO

This simple dish from la cucina di Sant' Arsenio makes a complete meal in less than 20 minutes.

1 pound spicy Italian sausage (5 large sausage links)
1 large onion, sliced
1 pound peppers (3 red, yellow, green peppers or a mix)
2 tablespoons olive oil
1 cup marinara sauce (see page 16)
Salt and crushed red pepper

1. Cut sausage in 1-inch pieces and sauté in olive oil for 3-4 minutes.
2. Add onion and sauté 5 more minutes.
3. Add peppers sliced in 3/8-inch strips and sauté 5 more minutes.
4. Add marinara sauce and salt and red pepper to taste and cook 5 more minutes over medium heat.

STEAK PIZZAIOLA

This recipe is great for London broil, round steak, and similar cuts of beef, since the acidity of the tomatoes tenderizes the meat. When buying round steak, be sure to select thin-sliced.

1-2 pounds of London Broil or thin-sliced round steak
4 tablespoons olive oil
1 tablespoon minced garlic
1 16-ounce can of crushed tomatoes
Salt and pepper

1. Trim the fat off the round steak.
2. In a large pot or sauce pan, sauté garlic in olive oil.
3. Add crushed tomatoes and cook 5 minutes to absorb the garlic's flavor.
4. Add slices of steak, salt and pepper to taste, cover, and cook for 15 minutes over medium heat.

Spizzotini ala Marco

Pop loved to transform an inexpensive, tough cut of beef into tender morsels with this recipe, and then announce to guests the cost of 62 cents per serving. Note that this dish requires one hour to prepare, but it's well worth the time so plan ahead.

1 pound stew meat
1 large onion, sliced and chopped
1 16-ounce can crushed tomatoes
4 tablespoons olive oil
Salt and crushed red pepper

1. Remove the fat and gristle from the stew meat and cut in bite-sized pieces.
2. Sauté onion in olive oil until golden.
3. Add the beef and cook until all the liquid evaporates (about 10 minutes).
4. Add a 16-ounce can of crushed tomatoes and salt and crushed red pepper to taste.
5. Reduce heat and cook 45 minutes, stirring occasionally to make sure it isn't burning.

SEAFOOD

CALAMARI MARINARA CAPITELLO

Capitello is the small seaside village (one hour south of Salerno) where Grandma and Pop spend their summers. This calamari dish only takes 10 minutes – as long as your marinara sauce is prepared in the fridge. The secret to delicious calamari is to avoid over-cooking.

1 pound calamari cut in bite-sized pieces (frozen or fresh)
4 tablespoons olive oil
1 tablespoon minced garlic
8 ounces white wine
1 cup marinara sauce (see page 16)
fresh parsley (optional)

1. Sauté garlic in olive oil.
2. Add calamari pieces and sauté until they turn white – only about 1 minute. Don't overcook!
3. Add white wine and cook for 1 minute.
4. Add salt and crushed red pepper to taste.
5. Add marinara sauce and cook over low heat for 5 minutes.
6. Serve over pasta cooked al dente.
7. Garnish with fresh parsley.

LINGUINI AL VONGOLE ALA DAVID

This dish is a delicacy, good beyond words, and takes only 15 minutes to make.

1 pound small fresh clams
1½ tablespoons minced garlic
3 tablespoons olive oil
¼ cup sherry or white wine
3 tablespoons chopped flat Italian parsley
½ pound linguine

1. Thoroughly rinse the clams two or three times in their shells to get all the grit off.
2. Sauté garlic in olive oil.
3. Add the wine, then the clams, and stir gently.
4. Cover, and cook about 5 minutes until the clams open.
5. Stir cooked pasta into the clam sauce.
6. Add chopped parsley and serve.

PESCE E PATATE ACQUAFREDDA

The combination of baked fish and potatoes is a regional favorite in this coastal town. The dish takes minutes to make. Acquafredda is a small town with a beautiful rock beach, the name of which literally translates to "cold water."

4 large filets of Tilapia (or other white fish)
4 medium potatoes
2 tablespoons olive oil
½ teaspoon oregano
1 cup Italian breadcrumbs
Salt and black pepper to taste

1. Preheat oven to 350° F.
2. Peel potatoes and slice about 1/8 inch thick.
3. Place half the potato slices in the bottom of baking dish sprayed with Pam.
4. Cover with half the olive oil, breadcrumbs, oregano, salt and pepper.
5. Add fish filets as the middle layer.
6. Add top layer of remaining potatoes.
7. Complete by covering with remaining olive oil, breadcrumbs, oregano, salt and pepper
8. Bake for 30 minutes, a little longer if you like crispy.

SALMON AMANTEA

This recipe transforms ordinary broiled salmon into a delicacy. It's worth the trip to the grocery store if you don't have Lemon Pepper in your spice rack. Trust me.

1 large salmon filet, 1-2 pounds
1 tablespoon lemon pepper
½ cup Italian bread crumbs
butter or margarine
Lemon juice (one lemon)

1. Cut salmon filet into 2-inch segments.
2. Put salmon pieces on broiling pan sprayed with Pam.
3. Squeeze juice from one lemon on top.
4. Sprinkle lemon pepper.
5. Add breadcrumbs on top.
6. Put small butter pad on top of each piece.
7. Broil for 10 minutes until pink.

SHRIMP FRANCESE CAPRI

This francese sauce is delectable. The secret is draining the oil after pan frying the shrimp, and then using butter to create the sauce.

1 pound large shrimp cleaned
1 cup flour
1 egg beaten
3 tablespoons vegetable oil
3 tablespoons butter
¼ cup white wine
Lemon juice (one lemon)
½ cup chicken broth
Salt and pepper

1. Butterfly the shrimp (split down the middle to fold open).
2. Dip in egg and dredge in flour
3. Pan fry in hot pan with vegetable oil, one minute per side.
4. Drain oil, add butter, wine, lemon juice, and chicken broth over shrimp.
5. Sprinkle in a little flour to thicken the sauce a bit.
6. Salt and pepper to taste, simmer 2-3 minutes, and serve.

SHRIMP SCARIO

This shrimp dish only takes 10 minutes if your tomato sauce is already made and waiting in your fridge.

1 pound shrimp
4 tablespoons olive oil
1 teaspoon minced garlic
1 quart tomato sauce
1 pound pasta, such as ziti

1. Wash and peel the shrimp and devein if they are large.
2. Sauté garlic in olive oil.
3. Add shrimp and sauté 2-3 minutes depending on size. Don't over-cook!
4. Add tomato sauce, salt and pepper to taste and simmer for 5 minutes.
5. Serve over pasta cooked al dente.

UNCLE TONY'S
SEAFOOD SALAD EXTRAVAGANZA

This is a family reunion treat, which is well worth the effort.

2 pounds shrimp
½ pound calamari (squid)
½ pound crabmeat (fresh, frozen or canned)
½ pound octopus (fresh, frozen or canned)
½ red onion chopped finely
2 stalks celery, use only the tender white side, chopped finely
½ bunch parsley, chopped; set aside a small handful of parsley chopped coarsely
1 cup olive oil
¼ cup white vinegar
1/8 cup lemon juice
Salt and white pepper to taste

1. Devein, cook and chop shrimp in large pieces.
2. Clean and slice calamari in ¼" rings and boil til tender, about 2 minutes – don't overcook.
3. Boil fresh crabmeat for 2 minutes and drain.
4. Clean and slice octopus in ½" pieces, boil til tender, about 3-4 minutes – don't overcook.
5. Mix all ingredients in a big bowl.
6. Mix in olive oil, white vinegar, lemon juice, salt and pepper.
7. Refrigerate overnight.
8. Toss before serving.
9. Garnish with fresh parsley.

DESSERTS

AUNT MARY'S APPLE PIE

This apple pie is proof that Aunt Mary inherited most of the baking genes in the family. Note that this recipe makes two pies – it's that good!

Ingredients for Crust:

4 cups of flour
1¾ cups shortening such as Crisco
1 tablespoon sugar
1 teaspoon salt
1 tablespoon white vinegar
1 egg beaten
¼ cup water

Ingredients for Filling:

12-14 apples peeled, cored, and sliced
½ cup sugar
1 heaping teaspoon cinnamon
¼ teaspoon nutmeg

1. Preheat oven to 375° F.
2. Mix flour for crust, shortening, sugar and salt with a spoon.
3. Separately mix egg, vinegar and water and mix into flour.
4. Let stand one hour.
5. For the filling, mix sugar, cinnamon, nutmeg and flour and then mix in apple slices.
6. Divide the dough into quarters and roll the dough about 1/8-inch thick.
7. For each pie, put the bottom crust in a pie dish and add half the apples.
8. Add the dough on top to cover the pie, pinch the crust edges together, and pierce the top crust with a knife to make 5-6 venting holes.
9. Bake for 45 minutes and let cool.

BISCOTTI ITALIANA ALA FLORA

This traditional Italian cookie is simply delicious and a treat for any occasion.

2 eggs, whisked
¼ cup softened butter
¼ cup honey
¾ cup brown sugar
½ cup white sugar
3 cups flour
1 teaspoon baking powder
1 teaspoon cinnamon
¼ teaspoon cloves
¾ cup almonds, toasted
and chopped

1. Preheat oven to 350° F.
2. Mix all ingredients together.
3. Knead and shape into 4 loaves.
4. Bake 20-25 minutes
5. Let cool enough to handle and slice with serrated knife in ½ inch slices on a diagonal.
6. Lay pieces on their side and toast 7 minutes.

BISCOTTI MARATEA

These hard cookies are a traditional Italian treat.

½ cup melted butter
2 small cups of demitasse coffee
Juice from one lemon
4 egg yolks
2½ cups flour
1 cup sugar
1 teaspoon vanilla extract
1 teaspoon baking powder

1. Preheat oven to 350° F.
2. Mix ingredients together.
3. Shape cookies any shape you like. For example, roll flat with a rolling pin and cut in rectangles, or use a cookie cutter.
4. Bake for about 10-12 minutes, depending on the thickness of the cookie.

BISCOTTI PER COLAZIONE

These breakfast biscuits have been a daily staple in Sant' Arsenio for generations.

¼ pound butter
3 large eggs
2½ cups flour
2 tablespoons baking powder
1 teaspoon vanilla
½ cup sugar

1. Preheat oven to 350° F.
2. Mix butter and sugar.
3. Add other ingredients and mix w/ electric mixer.
4. So the dough is soft but not sticky – maybe add flour if necessary.
5. Roll with rolling pin into rectangles of about 12 x 15 inches, about ½ inch thick.
6. Make little designs in the dough with a fork.
7. Cut in rectangles of about 1½ x 4 inches, about 12 per batch.
8. Bake for 35 minutes.

CARMELINA'S TORTA DI MELE (APPLE CAKE)

This delicious apple cake will make you a legend in your own time. Guaranteed foolproof.

2 eggs
1½ cup flour
1 cup sugar
1 teaspoon baking powder
1 teaspoon vanilla
5 apples
½ cup vegetable oil
½ cup lemon juice

1. Preheat oven to 350° F.
2. Peel and core apples and cut into eighths.
3. Mix apple slices in lemon juice and sprinkled sugar.
4. Mix other ingredients in loose dough and add apples.
5. Bake in a spring pan 35 for minutes until the top is golden.

BISCOTTI NENETTA

For children growing up in Sant' Arsenio, this cookie was a special treat for Easter.

12 eggs
1 cup vegetable oil
1 cup sugar
½ teaspoon baking powder
1 cup milk
Pinch of salt
Flour (as much as it takes)

1. Preheat oven to 350° F.
2. Mix eggs, vegetable oil, milk, sugar, salt and baking powder.
3. Add enough flour to make a soft dough and knead by hand.
4. Cover with a napkin and let rise one hour.
5. Roll out into the thickness of your little finger in "strings" about 6-7 inches long.
6. Shape into a small circle and "glue" the ends together with water or egg white.
7. Drop in boiling water and remove when it floats to the surface and let cool.
8. Bake for 20 minutes.

CARMELINA'S TORTA DI PERE

With this recipe you will discover that the only thing better than apple cake is pear cake.

2 pears, cut in slices
2 tablespoons baking powder
1 stick of butter
3 eggs
1 1/3 cups sugar
1 1/3 cups flour
Pinch of salt

1. Preheat oven to 350° F.
2. Beat butter and sugar until fluffy.
3. Add eggs, one at a time and beat.
4. Add flour, salt, and baking and beat.
5. Mix in the pear slices.
6. Bake in spring pan 40-45 minutes at 350° F. until the top is golden.

Nutella Cookies

If you haven't discovered Nutella, try this chocolate spread from Italy, which comes in a jar. These cookies are habit forming.

¼ pound butter
3 large eggs
3 cups flour
4 tablespoons Nutella
2 tablespoons baking powder
1 teaspoon vanilla
½ cup sugar

1. Preheat oven to 350° F.
2. Mix butter and sugar first.
3. Add the rest and mix with electric mixer.
4. Add Nutella and mix with spoon.
5. So the dough is soft but not sticky – add flour if necessary.
6. Wet hands with milk and shape into three little loaves, about 2" by 14".
7. Bake 40 minutes.
8. Let cool 10 minutes and cut with serrated knife into 5/8 inch slices.
9. Lay flat and bake for 15 minutes.

SOUR CREAM CAKE CORONA

This recipe, in tribute to the neighborhood in Queens where Grandma and Pop first lived in New York, will save you a trip to the Italian bakery for pastry for the holidays.

1 stick butter or margarine
¾ cup sugar
2 eggs
1 tablespoon baking powder
1 tablespoon baking soda
½ pint sour cream
1½ cup flour
1½ tablespoons cinnamon
½ cup sugar
½ cup walnuts

1. Preheat oven to 350° F.
2. Mix butter, eggs, sugar, sour cream, flour, baking powder and baking soda.
3. Put half the batter in a 9-inch square pan sprayed with Pam.
4. Sprinkle in half the walnuts and cinnamon.
5. Add the rest of the batter.
6. Spinkle in rest of walnuts and cinnamon.
7. Bake about 35 minutes at 350° F.

STRUFOLI PER NATALE

This traditional Italian treat for the Christmas holidays pays tribute to San Rufo, the small hilltop village next to Sant' Arsenio. This dessert is fun to make and great to nibble on.

6 eggs
8 ounces white wine
1 teaspoon salt
2-3 cups flour
5 cups vegetable oil
1 cup sugar
1 cup honey
2 ounces sprinkles

1. Mix eggs, white wine, and salt.
2. Add enough flour and mix to the consistency of bread dough.
3. Break off small handfuls and roll into "strings" (about 3/8 inch diameter (like bread sticks).
4. Line up the "strings" and cut with knife in little pieces about 3/8 inch.
5. Deep fry in very hot vegetable oil in deep sauce pan 1 minute until golden brown.
6. Scoop out with steel strainer, and place on paper towel.
7. Melt sugar and honey in large pan.
8. Add strufoli, stir with wooden spoon to coat.
9. Place on a serving dish and add sprinkles -- the tiny round ones are best.

TIRAMISU CLASSICO

2½ cups whipping cream, plus 2 tablespoons
6 egg yolks
1¼ cups sugar
8 ounces cream cheese, softened
¼ cup sour cream
3 (3-ounce) packages ladyfingers
4 teaspoons instant coffee granules
1 tablespoon brandy
2/3 cup hot water
2 tablespoons confectioner's sugar
½ teaspoon vanilla extract
2 teaspoons baking cocoa

1. Chill 1¾ cups cream in a metal bowl for 30 minutes.
2. Combine the egg yolks and sugar in a double boiler. Beat until thick and pale yellow. Place over boiling water, reduce heat. Cook for 10 minutes, stirring constantly. Remove from heat.
3. Beat the cream cheese with the sour cream and 2 tablespoons of whipping cream in a small bowl Add to the egg yolk mixture, beat until smooth.
4. Whip the chilled cream until soft peaks form. Fold into the egg yolk mixture. Set aside.
5. Line a greased springform pan with some of the ladyfingers.
6. Brush the ladyfingers with a mixture of the coffee granules, brandy and hot water. Spread with half the custard mixture. Top with the remaining ladyfingers. Brush with the remaining coffee mixture. Top with remaining custard.
7. Combine ¾ cup cream, confectioner's sugar and vanilla in a bowl, beat until soft peaks form. Spread over the tiramisu and then sift the baking cocoa over the top.
8. Chill 8 to 10 hours. Place on a serving dish, remove the side of the springform pan.

AFTER DINNER DRINKS

LIMONCELLO

This delightful after dinner drink is intended for sipping, not drinking. Beware, because the sugar and lemon mask its high alcohol content. Limoncello is also divine when drizzled on pound cake.

NOTE: This recipe takes 40 days to prepare, so plan ahead.

20 lemons
1 quart grain alcohol (or vodka, if grain alcohol is illegal in your state)
1 cup sugar
1 cup water

1. Peel 20 lemons with a potato peeler, saving only the yellow part of skin, not the white pith.
2. Put the yellow peeled skin into a quart of grain alcohol.
3. Store in a dark, cool place, such as a closet, for at least 20 days.
4. Boil water and add sugar to make a syrup the consistency of pancake syrup.
5. Let the syrup cool to room temperature.
6. Strain the alcohol mixture through a cheesecloth.
7. Add the cooled syrup to the strained alcohol.
8. Store the mixture for 20 more days.
9. Put the Limoncello in a glass bottle with screw cap or cork and store in the freezer.
10. Serve in cordial glasses. For a special treat, keep the glasses in the freezer.

CPSIA information can be obtained at www.ICGtesting.com
Printed in the USA
BVOW020120091211

277870BV00005B/1/P